BUILDING SELF-ESTEEM

By L.S. Barksdale

Second Edition

D1555070

The Barksdale Foundation
P.O. Box 187
Idyllwild, CA 92549

OTHER BOOKS BY L.S. BARKSDALE

Study Guide for Building Self-Esteem
Stress-free Living
Essays on Self-Esteem

Printed in the United States of America

First edition—140,500 copies

Second edition
First printing, February 1989, 2,500 copies. Second printing, July 1989, 7,500 copies. Third printing, December 1991, 5,000 copies. Fourth printing, October 1993, 5,000 copies. Fifth printing, October 1995, 5,000 copies, Sixth printing, April 1999, 5,000 copies.

Library of Congress Cataloging-in-Publication Data

Barksdale, L. S.
  Building self-esteem
  Bibliography: p.
  1. Self-respect. I. Title
BF697.5.S46B37   1989   158'.1   88-7661
ISBN 0-918588-11-1

Published by The Barksdale Foundation
P.O. Box 187
Idyllwild, California 92549
(909) 659-4676
Web site: http://www.barksdale.org

Table of Contents

ABOUT THE AUTHOR
AND
THE BARKSDALE FOUNDATION

Lilburn S. "Barks" Barksdale, born December 4, 1908, was raised on a cattle ranch in the Rocky Mountains and received his B.S. in Mechanical Engineering from Colorado State University in 1932. During the Depression he worked as a laborer and mechanic on various dam, road and tunnel construction jobs until the fall of 1935, when he landed his first engineering job. He opened his own engineering and development office in 1943 and became a pioneer in the design and manufacture of high pressure fluid controls for both aircraft and industry. In 1964 he disposed of his business interests in the U.S. and abroad to devote his energies to the furtherance of human understanding.

In spite of wide acclaim and material success, he suffered from many stress-related ailments and was never satisfied or "happy." Finally he realized that he did not feel "worthy" and that his underlying lack of self-esteem was the cause of his inability to enjoy life.

The following steps for building sound self-esteem are the fruit of his thirty-year search for inner peace and happiness. Mr. Barksdale was revising *Building Self-Esteem* at the time of his death. This edition benefits from his latest revisions.

The Barksdale Foundation is a nonprofit, self-funding educational organization devoted to enabling people to live happier, more care-free and productive lives. Self-esteem is recognized by authorities throughout the world as the root cause of personal and social problems. Mr. Barksdale developed a valid instrument for measuring self-esteem which has been used by people in the helping professions since 1972. This, together with the Barksdale Foundation's practical educational programs, enables people to accept themselves totally and unconditionally. The beneficial effects of this total self-acceptance (self-esteem) are lasting and dramatic.

The Foundation publishes Self-Esteem Programs for individual study, informal study groups, and professionally-conducted workshops. Barksdale Self-Esteem Programs are also offered at educational institutions, churches, mental health facilities, V.A. and other hospitals, prisons, and drug and alcohol treatment centers. For information about Barksdale Programs for Building Self-Esteem, and related materials for stress management, write or call:

The Barksdale Foundation
P.O. Box 187
Idyllwild, CA 92549
Tel: (909) 659-4676

FOREWORD

A WAY OF THINKING

by L.D. Mathae, Ph.D.
Consulting Clinical Psychologist

It seems strange to observers that so few people are happy, so few people enjoy life, and so few people know what to do about their situation. So many appear to have given up and to have reconciled themselves to unhappiness, so many live out their lives in "quiet desperation," and so very many attempt to lose themselves in various activities and pursuits.

But even stranger is the observation made by Schweitzer and others that few people *really think*—about themselves, their relationships, their life goals, and "what it's all about." Much of what passes for thinking in everyday life appears to be rationalization, blaming of one's fate or fortunes, projection, self-pity, or even a cleverly presented tirade of jealousy.

Tragically unheeded by many are such wise and timeless truths as the saying by Marcus Aurelius, "Very little is needed to make a happy life; *it is all within yourself, in your WAY OF THINKING.*"

To find a "way of thinking" that will help a person find "that type of fulfillment that will yield joy, serenity, wisdom, creativity, and power—that will enable him to resolve his own personal turbulences, achieve a deeper interdependence with his fellow man; and gain a sense of the end for which he was created" has been labelled the eternal search.

Philosophers, theologians, historians, writers, psychologists, and other professional observers of the human scene have searched deeply in this area; and have written profound volumes. Although such writings are by and large respected by the public, all too often an eager searcher begins a volume by one of them with high hopes; but after a few chapters turns away disappointed, with the feeling that the book is beautifully written, well-presented theory, is high and noble in tone, or dryly academic; but that, in short, it is not "practical," and fitted to everyday life. Further, many readers question whether or not the author has "really lived," been in the business "jungle," or has actually spent much time on life's "firing line."

Increasingly, the trend appears to be toward authors who have lived a full life, have "practiced" what they preached, and who now in their maturity have collected and organized for others the philosophies and principles they have lived by.

Such a person, in my opinion, is the author of this book, L.S. Barksdale. Here is a person of superb intelligence, deep insight, sincere compassion for his fellow human beings; who has "made it" in a competitive business world—a man who has been widely respected and honored by both fellow management and his employees; a person who has had the wisdom and integrity to operate an extensive modern business on "golden rule" principles. He has been widely acclaimed by professionals in many areas for demonstrating that fairness, honesty, sincerity, care and concern for the total welfare of his employees, and other so-called "old-fashioned" virtues are as timely and effective in a computerized business world as they were years ago.

His beliefs and writings are not wishful thinking, "pie in the sky" intellectualized theorizing, or still another form of "positive thinking" in a new guise. They are what I call "hardheaded humanism." His company policies were in full accord with the "latest" management theory of MIT's MacGregor and other researchers. Mr. Barksdale's observations, however, are not "academic" in flavor, but are rooted in real-life situations. His insights have been painfully gleaned from a "heap of living," emotional turmoil and a probing, analytical mind that has penetrated deeply into many lives—soul searching by many people.

With his background in engineering, Mr. Barksdale has had little use for unproven theories or pretty hypotheses. He has subjected his own operating principles and theories to the same rigorous testing that has made his hydraulic equipment world famous. He has carefully formulated his beliefs, subjected them to merciless analysis, taken them on life's proving ground, and has accepted his own thinking only when it consistently works.

His principles for living have contributed to his success and growth, not only in the business world, but also in his own personal life. They have enabled him to habitually experience an exceptional degree of psychological functioning and awareness, to have inner peace and happiness; and they have functioned as an emotional "shock absorber" in times of personal tragedy and adversity.

As a consulting clinical psychologist I have observed the actual effects and results of Mr. Barksdale's way of thinking and behaving toward his fellow human beings. It is most reassuring to note that his philosophies have produced an oasis of human-ness in the vast desert of dehumanization that is so typical of modern business—and some family living. His philosophies have created an atmosphere remarkably devoid of fear, deceit, withdrawal, and the other forces that can squeeze the creativity and very life of people doomed to live in an industrial jungle. To sum up my evaluation of Mr. Barksdale's principles—THEY WORK!

Although the founder and owner of three highly successful industrial firms, Mr. Barksdale became so convinced that better human understanding is of crucial importance in our troubled world that he disposed of his business interests in order to devote his energies to its advancement. It is his sincere hope and ardent desire that these same hard-won perceptions which have proven to be of such inestimable personal benefit to him be made available to others.

I am honored to present his writings, and gratified to know that excellent psychological principles are being interwoven with his own personal wisdom, and presented in a way that will be reassuring to many, and for still others will offer the first hope of a fuller life and a better world.

Building Self-Esteem

This book is not intended for casual reading. It is actually a workbook for those who are sufficiently unhappy with their present life style to spend the time and effort required to gain peace and happiness.

The material presented in this book will enable readers to cast off the false and destructive concepts, values, beliefs and assumptions that trap them in a quagmire of self-rejection. Condemnation, shame, guilt and remorse keep us from enjoying the beautiful and tantalizing "here and now"—the only living time there is. We hide, we repress, we try desperately to escape from what we perceive to be a chaotic, destructive and "evil" world. However, through conscientious study and implementation of this material you can achieve a much fuller, happier life.

If you are to attain the potential benefits, you must thoroughly study and thoughtfully question this material with as analytical and unprejudiced a mind as you can muster. It is packed with ideas vitally important to your well-being.

In order to evaluate the following concepts with an open mind, free of misconceptions and resistance, it is important to keep the following points in mind.

I propose no new system of belief or speculative philosophy. Despite any appearances to the contrary, I excuse no one from paying the price for self-destructive or antisocial behavior, since ignorance does not alter the adverse effects of one's hurtful acts, or relieve one of responsibility for any cause and effect relationships set in motion by such acts. I condone nothing; neither do I condemn nor make critical judgments. I do not propose what one should or should not do. I simply observe human behavior and report what I perceive to be its operating principles. These perceptions are based on years of study and observation, including a probing exploration and, to the best of my ability, an objective evaluation of my own and others' conduct.

The efficacy of the following ideas and techniques for increasing our individual awareness and building sound self-esteem have been thoroughly tested in my own life and in the lives of thousands of others. The results have conclusively shown that it *is* possible to achieve the tremendous benefits of sound self-esteem through this educational program.

Our Basic Need

Our basic need is to "feel good" about ourselves, mentally, physically and emotionally. This need is our ultimate motivation, for regardless of our immediate objective, everything we do is to achieve a sense of total well-being. Herein lies our crucial need for sound self-esteem, for we cannot possibly feel at peace with ourselves without significant senses of adequacy and self-worth.

All our goals, hopes and aspirations are based on this fundamental need. The more limited and distorted our awareness, the more misleading and unfulfilling are our efforts. For example, we drink, we smoke, we take drugs, we pursue and worship sex. We have compulsive needs for attention, to win, to be "better than," to avoid mistakes, to help others, to straighten people out, to accumulate wealth we can never use, to gain power and prestige, to eat all the rich expensive foods we can stuff into our stomachs, or whatever. We have a desperate urge to love and to be loved, to be accepted and approved of, to be respected and looked up to, on and on, ad infinitum. And, if we examine the ultimate motivation behind all needs, we find it is our universal need to *"feel good!"*

Thus, the true measure of success is the degree to which we actually do *"feel good"* about ourselves, despite material prosperity or prestige. Our only obstacle to achieving this ultimate objective is our limited and distorted awareness. The tests, of course, are our peace of mind and overall sense of well-being. This is what self-esteem is all about, for whether or not we realize it, practically our every endeavor is an indirect attempt to gain a sense of self-worth so that we can approve of and "feel good" about ourselves.

Life Can Be a Ball!

A happy, zestful life is, indeed, an attainable goal. It is not what happens to us but how we handle unwanted situations that determines our misery or well-being.

Our adverse experiences, handicaps and misfortunes are but the focal points for our pain and unhappiness. The actual cause of emotional suffering is how we perceive and react to unwanted circumstances. False and distorted perceptions, lack of understanding, warped needs and goals, and the unwise means by which we attempt to achieve those goals, produce our self-rejection and hurting. We can successfully deal with what is—not with what we wish or want.

The fundamental block to personal happiness and harmonious, loving relationships is a lack of awareness of the factors that influence our individual behavior. When these factors are scrutinized with a mind bent on discovering truth rather than confirming conditioned concepts, it becomes clear that antisocial and other harmful acts stem from a limited and distorted awareness, and the resulting pain of self-rejection.

Practically all human misery comes from self-rejection, the product of our limited and distorted awareness.

Awareness is the degree of clarity with which we perceive, understand and evaluate, both consciously and non-consciously, everything that affects our lives. Next to life and death, awareness is the most vital factor of human existence. It determines both our needs and how we fulfill them, how we feel toward ourselves, i.e., our self-esteem, and how we relate to our family and fellow human beings. In fact, our individual degree of awareness is the only limiting factor as to how wisely and harmoniously we act and react, both at work and at play. Thus, our awareness actually determines our degree of well-being, happiness and zest for living, for it is responsible for every choice, every decision we make!

Inadequate self-esteem is basically a problem of awareness. Self-rejection is the result of a mind that has been programmed, i.e., conditioned, by false and destructive concepts. This conditioning causes us to develop a life style that perpetuates our feelings of inadequacy, futility, and personal unworthiness. Adherence to distorted values generates a desperate and compulsive need to be "better than"—a compulsion that is behind our personal and social problems.

The Importance of Sound Self-Esteem

Self-esteem is literally a matter of life and death, for although we may continue to walk around and function in a purely minimal way, we are emotionally alive only to the degree that we accept the fact that we are each the most important person in our world, and that we exercise our innate authority to discharge our prime responsibility— that of our own development and well-being. Only through sound self-esteem can we eliminate the debilitating and disastrous senses of inadequacy and emotional turmoil that keep us from functioning in a harmonious and effective manner.

A healthy self-esteem is, therefore, absolutely essential to personal happiness and rich enjoyment of life. We may experience a fleeting elation over a happy event or sense of achievement, but lasting inner peace and happiness are possible only to the degree that we accept ourselves unconditionally—in spite of our human mistakes and failures.

When we stop denying and ignoring ourselves—when we are free to give precedence to our own needs and desires—we can become whole and independent beings. And, only to the degree that we acknowledge our unique importance and serve our basic needs, are we able and eager to concern ourselves with the needs of others, to be genuinely warm and loving, truly understanding and compassionate.

We cannot genuinely love others when we dislike or hate ourselves. The opposites of love and caring are isolation and indifference. Hate is an emotional involvement, actually a distorted love. Thus, when many of us follow Christ's admonition to "love our neighbor as ourselves," we literally hate our neighbor as we hate ourselves. How could governments sustain war if we actually did love our neighbor as ourselves? And, this is what we will do *automatically*, when we genuinely appreciate, accept, and feel warm and loving toward ourselves—when we achieve sound self-esteem!

Most doctors and psychologists accept the relationship between severe emotional turmoil and serious physical ailments. Parents, as role models, can generate the same calamitous results in their children.

The most damaging effect of low self-esteem is that it is passed from generation to generation, from great-grandparent to grandparent, from parent to child, ad infinitum, in a tragic chain reaction. Case histories document that suicidal tendencies also follow family lines. Low self-esteem contaminates our offspring like a deadly virus, for we are the models for our children. They quickly sense our lack of self-worth and are apt to think, "My parents are losers. How then, can I possibly be any good?" Parents, moreover, inculcate in their children the same false and distorted concepts, values and assumptions that generated their own self-rejection. Thus, our own low self-esteem may cripple the yet unborn unless we as parents take effective measures to break this vicious spiral.

Conscientiously building self-esteem is the way out of this disastrous dilemma. The more we perceive and understand the all-encompassing effects of low self-esteem, the more we will realize that self-rejection is actually the root of practically all our personal and social ills—divorce, alcoholism, suicide, drug addiction, and crime. On a global scale, it is responsible for the seeds of war itself.

Self-Esteem, What It Is Not

Self-esteem is not self love in an egotistical sense. In fact, self-praise and boasting are classic symptoms of low self-esteem, for if we truly accepted and appreciated our individual worth and importance, we

5

would have no need to boast in a vain effort to impress others with our ability and possessions.

Self-esteem is not an intellectual inventory of one's particular talents and capabilities, for in the eyes of the world one can be a great industrialist, a famous TV personality, a Barrymore, a Hemingway, a Marilyn Monroe or a Dylan Thomas, a champion in any sport or endeavor, a prized worker or craftsman—and still have a crippling lack of self-esteem. Indeed, history is crammed with cases in which the most intelligent and gifted people have become alcoholics or drug addicts, or committed suicide in order to escape from a self they have come to loathe.

Thus, one's self-esteem is not simply a matter of misery or happiness. It often is actually a matter of life or death, and if we do nothing to counteract our self-rejection, we usually feel worse as we grow older.

Self-Esteem, What It Is

Self-esteem, on a subtle and often unconscious level, is an emotion, how warm and loving you actually feel toward yourself, based on your individual sense of personal worth and importance.

Self-esteem is usually a subtle feeling that begins in childhood, and is continually reinforced by cultural conditioning. Fixed in our awareness for many years, it can be extremely difficult to change. Changing our feelings about ourselves entails a major revision of our awareness.

Sound self-esteem is rooted in unconditional acceptance of ourselves as innately worthy and important, despite mistakes, defeats and failures. This acceptance allows us to realize that we are each our own authority and to take active charge of our lives.

Low self-esteem results largely from the myth of perfection, i.e., the idea that since we possess free will, we should be perfect in all ways. Thus, we live with a haunting feeling that we are not really worthy, that somehow we should be or do better, even though we may not know exactly why or how.

Low self-esteem is the product of an accumulation of negative emotional reactions to experiences that have caused us to feel dependent and inferior. For example, parental attitudes that "a child should be seen and not heard," and "father/mother knows best," cause the child to feel too unimportant and unworthy to be treated with ordinary consideration and respect.

Our self-esteem not only colors our perception of our environment, it also plays a major role in our emotional reactions, moods and attitudes. For example, with low self-esteem we perceive ourselves to be inferior and unworthy, which makes it difficult for us to accept compliments, however sincere they may be. The tendency is to think that the donor is either stupid or hypocritical since we, ourselves, "know" we do not deserve it.

Self-esteem is not founded on an intellectual evaluation of one's character, personality or accomplishments. Instead, it is a deep and usually hidden feeling. In fact, relatively few people are aware of how they feel about themselves. Consequently, the surest way to determine our individual degree of self-esteem is to compare our behavior and personality characteristics to the behavior and characteristics of ideally high self-esteem, as we will do in the following evaluation.

Evaluating Your Self-Esteem

First, you will probably want to determine your current degree of self-esteem so that you can better tell how much time and effort is justified in improving it. As you continue you will find that sound self-esteem is indeed of crucial importance to your well-being and happiness.

It is important to clearly understand all statements and be completely honest in your scoring if you are to obtain a valid SEI (Self-Esteem Index). It is essential that you answer these statements according to how you actually *feel* or *behave*, instead of how you *think* you "should" feel or behave.

To obtain an indication of your prevailing self-esteem, score the statements as follows (each score shows how true *or* the amount of time you believe that statement is true for *you*):

0 = not at all true for me
1 = somewhat true *or* true only part of the time
2 = fairly true *or* true about half of the time
3 = mainly true *or* true most of the time
4 = true all the time

Self-Esteem Evaluation No. 69

Score

_____ 1. I don't feel anyone else is better than I am.

_____ 2. I am free of shame, blame and guilt.

_____ 3. I am a happy, carefree person.

_____ 4. I have no need to prove I am as good as or better than others.

_____ 5. I do not have a strong need for people's attention and approval.

_____ 6. Losing does not upset me or make me feel "less than" others.

_____ 7. I feel warm and friendly toward myself.

_____ 8. I do not feel others are better than I am because they can do things better, have more money, or are more popular.

_____ 9. I am at ease with strangers and make friends easily.

_____10. I speak up for my own ideas, likes and dislikes.

_____ 11. I am not hurt by others' opinions or attitudes.

_____ 12. I do not need praise to feel good about myself.

_____ 13. I feel good about others' good luck and winning.

_____ 14. I do not find fault with my family, friends or others.

_____ 15. I do not feel I must always please others.

_____ 16. I am open and honest, and not afraid of letting people see my real self.

_____ 17. I am friendly, thoughtful and generous toward others.

_____ 18. I do not blame others for my problems and mistakes.

_____ 19. I enjoy being alone with myself.

_____ 20. I accept compliments and gifts without feeling uncomfortable or needing to give something in return.

_____ 21. I admit my mistakes and defeats without feeling ashamed or "less than."

_____ 22. I feel no need to defend what I think, say or do.

_____ 23. I do not need others to agree with me or tell me I'm right.

_____ 24. I do not brag about myself, what I have done, or what my family has or does.

_____ 25. I do not feel "put down" when criticized by my friends or others.

_____ **YOUR SELF-ESTEEM INDEX (sum of all scores)**

To find your Self-Esteem Index (SEI), simply add scores of all self-esteem statements. The possible range of your Self-Esteem Index is from 0 to 100. Sound Self-Esteem is indicated by an SEI of

9

95 or more. Experience shows that anything under 90 is a disadvantage; a score of 75 or less is a serious handicap, and an SEI of 50 or less indicates a really crippling lack of self-esteem.

You may find comfort in the fact that lack of sound self-esteem is practically a universal problem that varies only in degree. It is, however, often so well camouflaged by false fronts and other protective devices that only a trained observer can detect it.

What Is Lack of Self-Esteem?

Self-rejection, a significant lack of self-esteem, is a *consciousness* that you are an unworthy, guilty and inferior human being—the automatic product of *our faulty cultural conditioning.* Self-rejection is the root cause of practically all personal and social ills.

Some Classic Symptoms of Low Self-Esteem

Typical Physical Characteristics: People who have one or more of the following characteristics: a wilted handshake; a weak, uncertain voice; a sloppy appearance; a humped, sagging posture; a turned-down mouth; lackluster eyes; a habitually tense, unhappy countenance; a reluctance or inability to meet another's direct gaze; definitely suffer from low self-esteem.

Common Personality Traits: People who are overly sensitive, prone to hurt feelings, timid, withdrawn and self-effacing or arrogant and domineering, aggressive and fiercely competitive; who wear protective masks, such as a synthetic jovial front; are prideful and boasting; who "come on" much too strongly or not at all; who are desperate for attention and have a compulsive need to dominate conversations; are compulsive perfectionists, confirmed "people pleasers" and name droppers; compulsive smokers, talkers, overeaters, drinkers, hobbyists, or professional "helper-outers"; those who are unable to pass up an opportunity to "straighten out" others; procrastinators; people who are impatient, harsh and demanding, excessively critical, who condemn both self and others; who are resentful and complaining; resist authority; are unable to admit mistakes and inadequacies; and lastly, those who try to make themselves "right" or "better than" by endeavoring to make others "wrong" or "less than," suffer from a crippling lack of self-esteem.

Some Psychological Characteristics: People who are anxious, vacillating and unsure of themselves, absorbed in their own problems and sense of inadequacy; who think of themselves as losers or "no damn good"; who are jealous, envious, and suspicious of others' motives; who dislike or despise themselves; who are ridden with shame, blame, guilt and remorse; who have an aching need for money, power and prestige; who have a desperate need to win, to be liked and accepted by everyone; who must be "right" every time; who have a compulsive need to fulfill others' expectations of them; have an aching hunger for recognition, approval and admiration—to love and be loved; to be respected for a "sterling character" and "achievements," for family, home and possessions; who live vicariously through sports heroes, TV and movie stars, through their children's accomplishments, mark themselves as having low self-esteem.

What Is Cultural Conditioning?

Cultural conditioning is the implanting of ideas, responses, and behaviors by repetition throughout a culture or society. A simple example of cultural conditioning is language. Through repetitious exposure to words correlated with ideas or objects, we each learn the language of the culture in which we live. Faulty cultural conditioning instills false ideas through repeated exposure. The idea that you could do better if you tried harder, or that you are bad if you do something that is bad are examples of faulty cultural conditioning. I'll show you why they are false a little later in this book.

Typical Sources of the Faulty Conditioning that Causes Self-Rejection

What causes our low self-esteem? The better we recognize and understand the sources of our low self-esteem, the better able we are to cope with this block to our happiness and peace of mind.

Most low self-esteem stems from unfortunate childhood experiences. The greatest gift we as parents can give our children is sound self- esteem.

Examples of How Parents and Other Authority Figures Handicap or Preclude Sound Self-Esteem

1. The destructive life style of low self-esteem parents is a model for their children. Low self-esteem parents have a compulsive need to find fault with everyone and everything—especially their spouse and children. Criticism and condemnation by parents, teachers and peers are the most common and destructive causes of low and crippling self-esteem. The reality is that children are neither their awareness nor their actions, and they can act *only* as wisely as their prevailing awareness permits.

2. Parents' and others' lack of recognition and appreciation of children as intrinsically valuable and important individuals, e.g., "a child should be seen and not heard," "Mother knows best," etc. result in children's needs, feelings, desires and opinions not being given due consideration.

3. A child's parents, family or friends make adverse comparisons with peers or a favorite brother or sister. These comparisons, combined with the child's own self-deprecating comparison with others of the same age who are admired for strength and ability, popularity, self-confidence or achievements, can overpower the child with a sense of inferiority and unworthiness.

4. Children feel inadequate when not encouraged to think for themselves, and motivated to be independent, to do what they can for themselves, to take responsibility for their needs and well-being to the extent of their ability to do so as they increase in age and experience.

5. The false concepts, values and reactions of parents, teachers and peers cause children to identify with their actions. For example, Johnny's mother, who has a severe migraine, calls him a "bad boy" because he slammed the door. In reality it was only his natural exuberance and lack of awareness of his mother's need for quiet that caused him to slam the door. Identification with our actions rather than recognition that our actions are but the means we choose to fulfill our needs, causes us to feel inadequate, unworthy and inferior or, worse still, loads us with self-condemnation, shame, guilt and remorse. Every time we make a mistake, we feel we should have done better.

6. Harsh and demanding parents set unreasonable standards, often raising them before their children have developed the ability to meet the present requirements. Parents may also subject their children to unreasonable, harsh criticism and undue and/or inconsistent punishment. Such actions cause early frustration, defeatism, and a destructive sense of inadequacy and inferiority.

7. Parents pushing children beyond their capacities in an attempt to boost their own low self-esteem through their children's achievements often causes children to develop deep feelings of inadequacy and unworthiness.

8. Rivalry and unsuccessful emulation of an extremely bright or gifted brother or sister, or of an exceptionally talented and prominent parent, often generate a deep sense of inferiority and inability to cope with life's problems.

9. A child's awareness of an unflattering physical appearance and/or "odd" apparel, plus perhaps physical, mental or emotional handicaps, damages self-esteem.

10. Raising children on the basis of "reward and punishment" rather than by motivating them through understanding, and allowing them the right to learn from their own mistakes, to accept and resolve their problems or suffer the consequences, undermines the child's sense of self-worth.

11. Accepting the deprecation and ridicule of others for the adverse economic, social, cultural or ethnic position of the child's family results in a sense of inferiority.

12. Over-possessiveness, over-permissiveness and over-control, exercised by one or both parents, nurture feelings of unimportance and low self-esteem in children.

13. An innate feeling of guilt is frequently induced by a sense of unfairness about parent's material wealth or affluent background.

14. Placing high values on money, achievement and *things* rather than on individuals and their innate worth and importance, can preclude or destroy sound self-esteem.

15. Repeated defeats and failures destroy children's sense of self-worth and result in the extremes of dropping out of school or society, or of becoming compulsive "over-achievers" in a desperate and futile attempt to prove their worth.

16. Parents condemning their children for procrastination and lack of self-discipline also generates a sense of guilt and unworthiness.

17. Lack of a sense of meaning and purpose in life seriously handicaps the achievement of sound self-esteem.

How We Perpetuate Low Self-Esteem

The following are significant factors of awareness that not only cause low self-esteem, but more importantly, ensure a crippling sense of inadequacy, anxiety and frustration. Recognition and understanding, however, make it possible to eliminate or revise these undesirable traits.

We perpetuate low self-esteem by:

1. Lack of faith, both in ourselves and in an ordered, beneficent and purposeful Universe;

2. Depending on others for a sense of importance and realness;

3. Not accepting our own authority and taking conscious charge of our lives;

4. Reacting instead of thinking and acting for ourselves;

5. Failing to recognize and exercise our innate authority to do anything we ourselves see fit, instead depending on others for what we can and need to do for ourselves, requiring their "permission," confirmation and agreement;

6. Adhering to false concepts, values and assumptions that engender condemnation, blame and guilt;

7. Identifying with our actions, not differentiating "who we ARE" from "what we DO"; indulging in self-blame, shame, guilt and remorse;

8. Value judging and resisting ourselves for not fully developing our inherent capabilities and talents;

9. Not allowing ourselves the right and freedom of full expression—to excel, to make mistakes, to "goof off," to fail;

10. Making comparisons with others a gauge of our own worth and importance, feeling we must "prove" ourselves "better than," not realizing that what another does or doesn't do has

no valid bearing on our own worth and importance; we each have our own unique talents and capabilities;

11. Neglecting to take any appropriate action within our capabilities, no matter how small or seemingly unimportant, for enhancing our sense of self-worth;

12. Resisting or being fearful and anxious about things we can do nothing about, instead of facing up to and accepting the reality of "what is";

13. Being impatient, harsh and demanding with ourselves.

Procedure for Building Self-Esteem

Since self-esteem is a *feeling* rather than an intellectual inventory of our assets, changing it entails a revision of the factors of our awareness that caused the feelings of inadequacy and inferiority.

The method we have developed has proven very effective for replacing these false and unsound factors of our awareness with sound concepts and then acting in accordance with the new concepts. The method consists of three separate and distinct steps, all of which are essential to our success in building sound self-esteem.

THE FIRST STEP: Expanding Your Awareness

As has been stressed earlier, increasing our awareness is crucially important, not only to building sound self-esteem, but also to enabling us to achieve more harmonious, effective and happier lives.

What We Mean by Awareness

It is essential to your understanding of the following principles of human behavior that you keep clearly in mind what we mean by "awareness." Remember, our AWARENESS is how clearly we perceive, understand and evaluate, both consciously and non-consciously, everything that affects our lives.

Its Nature: Our awareness is the *automatic* product of our heredity, i.e., everything we brought into the world with us, our Inner Knowing or intuitional insights, and our total life experience which has been directly responsible for all our conditioning. While our awareness is constantly being expanded by the cause and effect relationships we experience, if so motivated, we ourselves can deliberately increase it. We are all in the process of becoming more aware. However, at any given point in time our awareness is what it is—the automatic product of our heredity, our Inner Knowing and our total life experience. Thus, while it is indeed fortunate to have a high degree of awareness, logically one can no more take credit for it than he can be blamed for having a clubfoot. Conversely, neither has one any basis for embarrassment or shame because of an extremely limited and distorted awareness.

Everyone is unique in his or her degree of awareness, for no two people in the world have exactly the same heredity, Inner Knowing and total life experience. Thus, no one can be a valid reference as to what another "should" or "should not" be or do in any situation or

17

circumstance. We are each the beneficiary or victim, as the case may be, of our individual awareness. How wisely or unwisely we may act is completely determined by the relevant factors of our awareness, for it is the pertinent factors of our awareness that determine our every choice. To the degree that our perception and understanding of "what is" are limited and distorted, will our needs and actions be distorted, inappropriate and destructive.

Its Scope: "Awareness" is a very comprehensive term. It incorporates many factors, including everything we perceive with our five senses as well as everything we perceive instinctively and intuitively, both consciously and non-consciously. It is the product of the conditioning of our entire life experience and our innate intelligence and intuition. Our awareness is responsible for our insights, inner urges, emotional reactions, and every decision we make.

Our awareness includes the following specific factors:

1. Our intellectual acumen, our individual ability to observe, analyze, correlate and evaluate all experience, both negative and positive, and to accurately anticipate the total cost and benefits of any decision or action we might take;

2. Our Inner Knowing or intuitional insights, and our instinctual and subconscious drives and urges;

3. Our total conditioning, both conscious and non-conscious, resulting from our entire life experience from birth to the present instant, for it is our total life experience that has formed our concepts, assumptions, values, ideals, beliefs, convictions, learned knowledge, memories, skills, etc.;

4. The effects of our conditioning: our moods, attitudes, emotional reactions, prejudices, habits, desires, fears, aspirations, goals and, most important of all, how we feel deep down about ourselves, our sense of personal worth and importance in the scheme of things.

Roadblocks to Increasing Your Awareness

To the degree that the following conditions are true for you, you will experience difficulty in consciously expanding your awareness:

1. Reluctance or fear to accept responsibility for your own life and well-being;

2. Insufficient motivation to spend the necessary time and effort to increase your awareness—lack of recognition of the crucial importance of increased awareness to your inner peace and happiness;

3. Resistance to new ideas and change—a conditioned plane of reference, a biased, closed and rigid mind;

4. Inability to recognize and accept your innate authority to examine and question accepted values, concepts and assumptions, and then draw your own conclusions;

5. Self-condemnation and recrimination that prevent a deep probing into your emotional reactions and mistakes, into your distorted needs and unacceptable motivations.

Revising Your Concepts of Human Behavior

Personally, I am deeply convinced of the truth of the following concepts. I perceive them to be the actual operating principles of human behavior. However, if they are to be meaningful, and therefore, of significant benefit to you, it is essential that you conscientiously check their validity in your own behavior and that of your associates.

Before we proceed with our investigation, it is vital to have a clear understanding of just what we mean by "motivation" since everything we do hinges on our *motivation.*

Contrary to popular opinion, everyone is always motivated, for we can do nothing we are not motivated to do. Everyone, sick or well, active or lazy, *is* motivated. For example, the man dozing in the sun is motivated to sit and doze in the sun. Otherwise he would be doing something else. We can do only what we are motivated to do, consciously or non-consciously. We cannot even get up out of a chair unless we are so motivated.

What We Mean By Motivation: To be "motivated" is to want to do a specific thing more than we want to do anything else at that particular time. Even though we may not be aware of the specific desire, motivation is what we most want to do in the sense of "what we would rather do than not do." If we probe deeply enough into our own and others' specific actions, provided that we can withhold all value judgments during the process, we find that there is simply no other reason possible for doing anything, even though we may not always be aware of it.

There are many things that motivate us. Probably the greatest handicap to understanding motivation is our conditioned concept that we "want" to do only what we find pleasure in doing, what we "enjoy" doing. Such is not the case.

Let us look behind "motivation." When we do so it is apparent that every human act is a response to a personal need or desire. Our basic need is to be comfortable, mentally, physically and emotionally—to enjoy a sense of inner peace and well-being. Thus, our fundamental motivation, in a total sense, is to "feel good," or at least to feel as good as the existing conditions will allow.

To go a step further, it is also apparent that our unfulfilled needs generate tensions. Thus, to "feel good," i.e., to feel comfortable, we must resolve or satisfy these tensions. Such tensions may be generated by fear, cold or pain; our hunger for food or sex; our need for attention, to win, to succeed; our need for confirmation and agreement, for acceptance and approval, to be liked or loved; our fear of what others may think or say; or any type of force or coercion. For example, I may have a strong value against bearing arms and killing my fellow human beings. If, however, I am faced with the alternative of personal disgrace or going to prison, or possibly getting shot, I might well be motivated to bear arms. The deciding factor would be my willingness or unwillingness to pay the price demanded for not going to war.

Unless I perceive how I can benefit my particular need by the proposed act or endeavor, I will continue with what I am currently doing. For instance, for me to get out of bed in the morning, I must perceive that by doing so I am fulfilling a personal need. My need may be to get some food in my stomach, to meet my personal commitment to be active and productive, to keep from losing my job, or simply to maintain the approval of my neighbors. Normally, of course, I operate under several nonconflicting motivations at any given time, such as the desires to achieve material success, improve my golf game, and please my wife.

In the final analysis, motivation is simply a matter of perceiving that the potential benefits of a given action outweigh the price demanded, and that the action is the most desirable alternative available for meeting the need in question. Most personal confusion and conflict stem from not clarifying our motivation, from not making a complete decision to pay or not to pay the price demanded for our competing desires.

To *change* our motivation, we must first become aware of either a greater need or a more beneficial means of fulfilling our existing need. Such a change in our awareness may come about through our own or others' efforts, or simply through the force of circumstances. It is essential, however, that if the change is to come through our own conscious efforts, we ourselves have the awareness to be motivated to make such efforts. To say one should or should not do a certain thing is, therefore, quite meaningless if the individual does not have the awareness to be so motivated.

Now, here are the concepts, or as I see them, the relevant facts of human behavior.

The Realities of Human Behavior

Note: A clear understanding of the following concepts is the single most important requirement for building sound self-esteem.

1. Every human act is a response to a personal need. The more intense the need, the more intense the response or motivation.

2. Our ultimate or basic need is to "feel good," to have a satisfying sense of worth and innate importance, regardless of our mistakes and what others may say or think of us.

3. Both our needs and their intensity are determined by our current state of awareness.

4. Our actions are but the *means* we choose to fulfill our needs. Such means are determined by our awareness.

5. Inspection discloses that we are each solely responsible for our own life and well-being. We, therefore, have the innate authority to do whatever we see fit.

6. There is, however, a *price* exacted for everything we do, refuse or neglect to do. If we are to act harmoniously, we must know the price in order to decide intelligently if we are able and willing to *pay* it.

7. The price we pay for our actions is determined by the unwanted consequences of our proposed act, including any expenditure of time, money, emotional and/or physical energy, plus any foregoing of competing needs and desires.

8. Although we can do anything we want, what we most want, what we would rather do than not do, i.e., our *motivation*, is determined by our awareness.

9. A searching examination of our actions discloses that we can do only what we are *motivated* to do, i.e., only what we would rather do than not do. There is no other reason possible for doing anything!

10. Our exercise of "free will" is, therefore, limited to what we or others can motivate ourselves to do.

11. Since our motivation is determined by our awareness, and since we can do only what we are motivated to do, everything we do is literally *dictated by* our awareness.

12. Moreover, since we can do only what we most want to do, "will power" is *per se* nothing more or less than "desire power," actually an intensified motivation. For example, if we try to stop smoking and fail, it is not because of "weak wills," but because our "will power" to smoke is so strong that it outweighs our desire to stop smoking.

13. Now, although our awareness is in a continual state of change, at the instant of any decision it is "what it is"—as fixed and rigid as a steel bar.

14. And, since our awareness determines our motivation, at any given instant there is one and only *one* decision we can possibly make.

15. Therefore, we all do the only thing we can possibly do at the time, for we can do only what our prevailing awareness dictates.

16. Thus, we all do the *best* thing we can possibly do at that particular instant.

17. Although we don't have to like what we or others do, and even though an action may not be "right" or "fair," there is absolutely no rational justification for condemnation, shame, blame, guilt or remorse, for *no one* can do better than his "best."

18. Furthermore, all moral admonitions, all "oughts," "shoulds" and "musts" are irrelevant to our conduct if our prevailing awareness does not allow us to comply. For example, to "know better" is not sufficient to cause us to "do better" if

we have a conflicting need that outweighs an accepted value to "do better."

19. Likewise, there can be no valid justification for punishment as such (or for pride or reward), for our awareness is but the automatic product of our heredity, Inner Knowing, and total life experience. It simply is what it is at the time of any action. Thus, we all do what we "have to do" at the time, be it "good," "bad" or indifferent.

20. Moreover, since we can do only what our prevailing awareness dictates, there is no logical basis for psychological resistance and resentment of an unwanted situation or another's conduct. Although we do not have to like it, and although it may not be "right" or "fair," it IS the REALITY of the moment—*no other* action is possible at that time for that individual.

21. Inspection also discloses that we are not our "actions"; we are "that which acts." Our actions are but the *means* we choose to fulfill our needs.

22. Thus, we are not "bad" because we act "bad." We are but the victims of our limited or distorted awareness. (Johnny is not a "bad" boy because he slams the door when his mother has a headache. He is simply not sufficiently aware.)

23. Everyone has the innate authority and freedom to make mistakes, for although we are responsible for our individual well-being, we can do only as well as our prevailing awareness motivates us to do.

24. Furthermore, since we are not our actions, there is no justification for feeling ashamed, guilty, or "less than" for our mistakes.

25. From the foregoing statements, it is evident that there *is* a rational basis for empathy and compassion for those who act

in an unwise or hurtful manner, regardless of how injurious their actions prove to be.

26. Since we can do only what our awareness permits us to do, there are only "wise" and "unwise" acts.

27. Consequently, the terms "good" and "evil" are simply reflections of one's current state of awareness.

28. Nevertheless, no matter how limited and distorted our awareness, we are each inescapably responsible for our actions, both wise and unwise, for we inevitably benefit or suffer according to the consequences of our every act.

29. It is evident that we are not our awareness, that we are that which is aware. Therefore, no one is "bad," intrinsically less worthy, or inferior for having an extremely limited and distorted awareness.

30. The foregoing facts indicate that although we are all in varying states of awareness, in different stages of learning and growth, regardless of nationality, race, creed or color, we are all intrinsically *equal*.

31. It follows that everyone's prime responsibility is learning and growing—the expansion of one's individual awareness, for we each invariably profit or suffer according to the wisdom or lack of wisdom in our every thought and action.

32. Our only limitation is our *limited* awareness!

How About the Consequences?

It is not always apparent that one "suffers" the consequences of antisocial and hurtful acts. One can, in fact, betray his wife or friends, gyp his neighbors, swindle the public, take advantage of widows and orphans, and commit various nefarious acts, and seem to get away "scot-free." Such, however is not the case.

We do not have to observe the law of compensation—"It is done unto us as we do unto others"—to know that we inevitably pay the price for our injurious acts to others.

As stated earlier, our basic need is to "feel good" about *ourselves*. Human beings are so constituted that it is impossible for us to "feel good" about ourselves when we knowingly injure another. We may refuse to recognize our hurtful act, to "harden our heart," and turn off our conscience. Everyone, however, is innately good and has a deep urge, however hidden, warped or beaten down, to be "godlike," to express goodness and love.

When this drive is thwarted through a limited awareness and a misdirected need to "feel good," our conscience goes underground and gnaws at self-worth and the obscured sense of rightness, thus keeping us from enjoying the fruits of injurious acts. With the ability to "feel good" about ourself long since gone down the drain, we pay and pay an ever increasing price in emotional turmoil, self-disgust, and loathing as misdeeds mount in a continuing attempt to achieve fulfillment of the distorted need for money, power and prestige—for approval and acceptance—actually, the desperate need to "prove our worth" in order to become acceptable *in our own eyes*.

Increasing Your Awareness through Self-Exploration

If so motivated, you can greatly enhance your awareness by considering yourself a "human research laboratory," and then exploring your every experience and reaction to see what it can yield toward self-discovery—by accepting the challenge to learn who you *are,* and how and why you function as you do. Once you actually become seriously involved in self-exploration, you will find there is no adventure more exciting or more rewarding! You will never become bored if you maintain an active interest in self-discovery.

The most fruitful areas for self-exploration are your thoughts, speech and desires; your actions and the needs which generated them; your inner urges and compulsive drives; your emotional reactions; your moods and attitudes and what triggered them; your values, concepts and assumptions.

Prerequisites for Self-Exploration

The *first requirement* for rewarding self-exploration is to recognize, accept and exercise your *own* innate authority, to question EVERY-THING and to draw your own conclusions, based on the available evidence.

The *second requirement* for successful self-exploration is to stop all self-recrimination and condemnation—to refuse to accept any blame, shame or guilt, regardless of what undesired characteristics or motivations you discover in yourself. Otherwise you would become too uncomfortable to proceed with your inner search, for you would then "turn off," deny, rationalize, lie or create alibis in order to avoid the discomfort of honest self-inquiry. You would thus be unable to probe deeply enough to find significant answers. Only when you feel completely free to confront yourself, despite your unwise or "despicable" actions, only when you are aware that you have always done the best you possibly could at the time, regardless of the magnitude of your mistakes, can you truly discover how and why you act and react as you do. Only then can you make meaningful progress in expanding your awareness.

The *third requirement* for productive self-exploration is to program yourself to maintain an awareness of yourself, of your thoughts, speech, needs, actions, emotional reactions, moods and attitudes.

General Procedure for Self-Exploration

1. Observe, question and think.

2. Analyze, correlate and evaluate.

3. Draw your own conclusions.

4. Confirm your conclusions by checking and rechecking them against observable facts, both now and later.

Explore the following:

1. **Your Thoughts and Mental Images:** If you are to take charge of your life, you must be conscious of your thoughts and mental images, for all action is preceded by a thought and an image, conscious or not. What are the needs and desires, the fears, hopes and aspirations, the values, concepts and assumptions behind your thoughts and mental images? What initiated your thoughts and where are they leading you?

2. **Your Speech:** Everything you say is significant, probably much more than you realize. Watch what you say. Ask yourself, "Why did I say that?" Was it a request for information or advice? Was it to impress, to boast? Was it a demand for confirmation, or was it simply to share an opinion or some interesting information? Was it your hunger for approval and acceptance? Was it to belittle, criticize or condemn another? Was it a veiled plea for help, or perhaps a threat? Was it to express joy, anger, hate, resentment? Did it indicate envy, jealousy, suspicion or whatever? In other words, what is the need behind everything you say? Examine any nonroutine speech honestly and carefully, no matter how "bad" or "unacceptable" you may consider it to be.

3. **Your Needs, Desires and Objectives:** Your needs, desires, objectives and their implications can perhaps tell you more about yourself than any other areas. Examine them honestly and carefully in a manner similar to the method outlined above for exploring your speech. Are your needs, desires and objectives valid? Are they distorted, based on false values, concepts or assumptions? Are they constructive or destructive? Where will they take you? What are your life goals and aspirations? Will fulfillment of a particular need be compatible with them? Do your proposed actions contribute to your life's objectives?

4. **Your Actions and Motivations:** What are the needs and desires behind your actions? Why did you just do as you did? What was your apparent motivation? What was your real motivation? Is the proposed action the best alternative available for meeting your current need? Exactly why do you act or react differently to your spouse, sweetheart, boss, janitor, servant, waitress, clerk, minister, a prominent public figure, your fishing buddy?

5. **Your Emotional Reactions:** Your emotional reactions can be most revealing if you will take the time and effort to honestly examine them. Remember, however, that you must first stop all value judging if you are to achieve optimum results. Just why did you become angry, hurt, resentful, excited, "up tight," etc.? What is the basis for your disappointment, frustration, conflict, shame, pride, resistance, resentment, rebellion; for your joy, happiness or relief? Get in touch with yourself through recognizing and accepting the reality of your emotions. Do not hide, ignore or repress them. What do they tell you about your concepts, values, beliefs and assumptions? What triggers them? Do you repress or express your emotions? Why?

6. **Your Moods and Attitudes:** Explore these in a manner similar to the way you explore your emotional reactions. Just why are you exhilarated, tense, depressed, confident, nervous, enthusiastic, apathetic, joyful, arrogant, cooperative or uncooperative, proud, judgmental, defensive, cynical or subservient? Why are you rebellious, resistant, antagonistic and hostile, anxious, fearful, hateful, kind and loving, unhappy, sad, aggressive, friendly, open or suspicious, accepting, calm, optimistic, domineering, critical and condemnatory? Why do you feel vulnerable, "put down," insulted, "less than," betrayed?

7. **Your Values, Concepts, Beliefs and Assumptions:** Exploration of the preceding items has no doubt revealed your

values, concepts, etc. Your job now is to carefully examine and check them against observable reality. Are they valid or invalid? Why? Have you made them yours by a probing examination, or were they uncritically accepted from your parents or others? Remember, we can cope only with reality. False and unreal concepts, values and assumptions cause nothing but problems and heartache.

8. **Your Mistakes and Defeats:** Ask yourself, "Where did I go wrong? How can I do better next time? What are the pertinent factors? Are these factors within my control? Do I allow myself to make mistakes without self-recrimination, guilt and feeling 'less than'? If I cannot, why?"

9. **Your Problems:** The first questions to ask yourself are, "Is this really *my* problem or am I taking on someone else's problem? If so, why?" You need to define the problem before you can solve it. What is the origin or basis of the problem? What are the pertinent factors? What can you learn from it? Are you perhaps trying to deal with symptoms rather than causes?

10. **Your Compulsions:** All compulsive actions are indicative of faulty conditioning and are a prime symptom of a crippling self-esteem. Ask yourself, "Why am I compulsive about this? What specific conditioning is responsible for this compulsive action? How can I stop it? Are any compulsive actions justified? Why can I not choose to act simply on the merits of a proposed action?"

11. **Your "Oughts," "Shoulds" and "Musts":** Nothing will throw more light on your concepts, values and assumptions than these terms. Analyze such terms in the context in which they are used to see how relevant and significant they are. Remember, we can only do what we "should," "ought" or "must" if we are motivated to so act. Otherwise, such admonitions only serve to create confusion, conflict, frustration and guilt. In the ultimate analysis, just who is responsible

for you? Who is your authority? Who but you has the right to direct and control your life? Even your boss is but exercising the authority you delegated to him when you accepted your job and, if *you* are willing to pay the price, you can withdraw such authority any time *you* see fit.

12. **Your Physical Tensions:** What is the origin of your tension headache, ulcer, backache? How can you resolve the problem and release the tension?

Certainly the more we strive to know and understand ourselves, the greater will be our awareness of human behavior, and thus the more gentle, kind and loving we will be to both ourselves and others.

Increasing Your Awareness
Through Outside Sources

Investigating Your Environment

To the degree that you are alert, observant and curious about your total environment, and especially the individuals you contact in your day-to-day activities, you will expand your awareness outside yourself.

Why do certain people react to you as they do? What needs do their actions and conduct indicate? What is their state of awareness, their degree of self-esteem? Why do you react to them as you do? Why do you dislike some, like or have a neutral reaction to others? What can you learn from specific experiences, situations and social conditions? What "good" can come from resisting and resenting things you cannot change? What "bad"?

Motion Pictures, TV, Plays, etc.

If you carefully watch and question the players' actions and reactions, their attitudes and prejudices, you can heighten your awareness comparable to what you can by observing and questioning the actions of real-life individuals, perhaps even more, for you can often see such situations in a better perspective.

Books, Lectures, etc.

These are excellent sources for increasing your awareness if you will but explore the ideas presented with a free and open mind—if your motive is to learn rather than pass judgment. In the appendix of this book is a partial list of thought provoking books for expanding your awareness.

Who Am I?

A sculptor, asked how he sculpted such a beautiful elephant, answered, "I just chipped away all the marble that did not look like an elephant." In a similar way we can perhaps find our real selves by eliminating what is not truly us. Let us examine the possibilities.

Am I my actions? No, I am not my actions; I am that which acts. My actions are but the means I choose to fulfill my needs. Actions are just manifestations of my prevailing awareness, for both my needs and how I choose to fulfill them are determined by my awareness.

Am I my body? No, I am not my body, for I can lose both arms and legs, as well as many other parts, without being diminished as an individual. My body is merely the instrument or means through which I function in this material phase of my existence. Even though my body be wasted away to the point of death, I am still *me*—as much as I ever was.

Am I my mind? No, I am not my mind, for my mind is but a human computer that receives the data of my five senses. My mind is the instrument through which my awareness functions.

Am I my awareness? No, I am not my awareness. I am that which is aware. My awareness is but the automatic product of my heredity, Inner Knowing, and total life experience, including my total conditioning and the impact of my environment. My awareness acts as my deputy self, my commander-in-chief, for I function through awareness. If I *were* my awareness, I would cease to be every time I fell into a dreamless sleep.

Am I my ego? No, I am not my ego. My ego is but my innate drive to fulfill my basic need, my fundamental need to "feel good," physically, mentally and emotionally. My ego responds to the tensions generated by my desires, no matter how distorted or destructive such desires may be as a result of my limited and often distorted awareness. The better I feel toward myself and my environment, the less need for my ego to manifest itself.

Then what am I? I am a unique and precious being, a nonphysical essence. My awareness tells me, "I am"—of this I have no doubt. Therefore, I must be a nonphysical essence, a part of all Life. My awareness shows me that I am unique, for no one has exactly the same heritage, background and awareness as I. All my experiences, especially my problems and mistakes, are continually adding to my awareness. Since life is of ultimate importance, *I am* a unique and precious being, ever learning and growing. The greater my awareness, the greater is my capacity for love and enjoyment of life. The more richly I enjoy life, the more eager and able I am to contribute to the well-being of those around me.

Putting It All Together

The diagram on the following page is a graphic representation of the concepts we have been exploring. When you thoroughly comprehend its content, you will have completed the first step for achieving sound self-esteem—understanding the realities of human behavior.

The basic premise for building self-esteem is that we are *not* our body, mind, actions or awareness. We *are* each the precious, nonphysical essence or spirit that animates our mind and body. Our body is simply the vehicle which houses us and does our bidding. Our mind is our brain, or human computer, and its associated nervous system. Our actions are simply the means we choose to satisfy our individual needs, and the means we choose to fulfill our needs are determined by our individual awareness.

The Human Behavior Diagram indicates how we actually function. Our "awareness" is without doubt the most important factor in human behavior. As stated before, our *AWARENESS* is how clearly we see and understand, both consciously and non-consciously, *everything* that affects our life. We are not our awareness; we are the individual who is aware—we certainly cannot *be* "how clearly we see and understand." As indicated on the diagram, our awareness is the *automatic* product of our *HEREDITY*, everything we brought into the world with us; our *INNER KNOWING*, or intuitional insights; and our *TOTAL LIFE EXPERIENCE*, including the lifelong impact of our *ENVIRONMENT*.

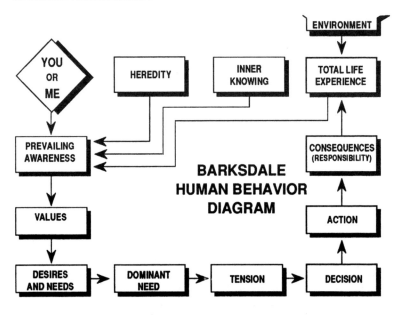

VALUES are what we feel are of significant worth and importance to us personally—they are tangible or intangible, sound or distorted, depending on the degree to which our awareness is in alignment with reality, with what actually IS. Our needs are personal *DESIRES* so strong that if they are not fulfilled or resolved, they generate uncomfortable tension. Our *DOMINANT NEED* is the need on which we act. *TENSION* is our signal to act in order to free ourself of discomfort, for our fundamental human need is to "feel good," (an overall, satisfying sense of inner peace and well-being) mentally, physically and emotionally.

The basic law of human behavior is: "We can do only what we would rather do than not do at the time." There are no exceptions to this law, because there is no other reason possible for doing anything. Therefore, in order to relieve our tension, we determine what we "would rather do than not do" and make a *DECISION* to take *ACTION*. We inevitably do what our prevailing awareness determines "we would rather do than not do" because we are unwilling to accept the consequences of doing otherwise. For example, suppose you really hate to get up in the morning and go to work, yet you realize you would lose your job if you didn't. You really need the money to support your family, consequently you *want* to get up and go to work because you would rather do so than lose your job, even though you may not *enjoy* doing so.

Since "what we would rather do than not do" is determined by our *prevailing* awareness, by how clearly we see and understand everything that affects our lives at any point in time, it is now apparent that our prevailing awareness determines everything we feel, think, say and do—everything we do, refuse, or neglect to do.

Our every action produces *CONSEQUENCES*. The consequences of everything we do, refuse or neglect to do make us *inescapably responsible* for everything we feel, think, do and say, for we benefit or suffer, "feel good" or "feel bad," depending on the consequences of our actions. According to Webster's dictionary, the true meaning of responsibility is "answerable to or accountable for."

The consequences of our every act feed into our prevailing awareness by way of our total life experience, giving us a new awareness which provides new data with which to satisfy future dominant needs. Our awareness may also be changed by new input from our

Inner Knowing, our direct connection with our Source. Our Inner Knowing is the infallible wisdom ever waiting on the threshold of our consciousness. However, at any point in time, our awareness simply is *what it IS*, the *automatic* product of our Heredity, Inner Knowing, and Total Life Experience, none of which factors can we change on demand.

The fact that the data supplied by our individual awareness determines everything we feel, think, say and do; and that at any given time our awareness simply is what it IS, makes it apparent that there is no rational justification for blame and guilt. In other words, any fault in what we do lies not in us but in our prevailing awareness, which is not us and for which we are never to blame.

Our individual awareness is unique, for no two people, not even identical twins, can have the same Heredity, Inner Knowing and Total Life Experience. We assume others have the same awareness as we do and, therefore, that they "should" act as *our* unique awareness indicates *we* would. What IS the reality? The reality is that they can do only what *their* unique awareness motivates them to do, i.e., what it determines "*they* would rather do than not do" at the time. It is, therefore, unrealistic to expect others to behave as our individual awareness indicates they "ought" or "should." As stated before, we can do only "what *we* would rather do than not do"—and this is determined by our unique awareness, while others' behavior is determined by their unique awareness.

Our awareness has been distorted, i.e., thrown out of alignment with reality, with what actually IS, by the false and destructive concepts of who we are and why we behave as we do. These unreal concepts have been laid on us from birth by our faulty cultural conditioning. One such false concept is that we *are* our actions and awareness. This concept causes us to *value judge* and *resist* ourselves and others for unwanted behavior.

A value judgment is condemnation of anyone or anything we do not like or want because it does not satisfy or comply with our individual values, desires or expectations. Resistance is an emotional *unwillingness* to accept anyone or anything we do not approve of or want. We automatically resist what we do not like or want.

Our *fundamental human need is to "feel good"* mentally, physically and emotionally. We resist people we do not like or approve of because we perceive them to be a threat to our "feel good" and we mistakenly believe that anything we do not like or want keeps us from "feeling good." What is the reality? The reality is that it is not what we don't like or want that causes us to "feel bad"; it is our *emotional resistance* to the reality that it actually exists that destroys our "feel good" by generating hurting emotions which result in destructive stress.

A *consciousness* that we are not our bodies, personal characteristics, actions or awareness—that we are inviolable spiritual beings, totally worthy and without fault just as we are—enables us to accept ourselves and others totally and unconditionally, regardless of unwanted characteristics or behavior. When we do so, we automatically feel warm and loving toward one another, for love is a *natural* state of being.

To actually experience love, however, we must first remove the impassable barrier to loving and being loved that we erect by value judging and resisting each other. The observable reality is that we cannot experience love when value judging and resisting ourselves and others, because our emotional resistance generates such negative, hurting emotions as hostility, resentment, anger, hate and bitterness.

Value judging and resisting ourselves makes us feel unworthy and "less than," and results in a compensating need to value judge and resist others, which generates a compensating need in them to value judge and resist us in return. This cycle of mutual value judging and resisting erects the "impassable barrier" that denies genuinely loving relationships. This is the reason that we can love others only to the degree we truly love ourselves, for only to the degree that we stop value judging and resisting ourselves can we rid ourselves of a compensating need to value judge and resist others.

It is, however, vitally important to realize that we do not have to like, approve or "put up with" unwanted behavior in order to accept the individual totally and unconditionally. Such acceptance of people, but not necessarily their unwanted actions or behavior, enables us to deal with them and their behavior as harmoniously and effectively as circumstances permit, for we will not then be experiencing emotional turmoil and destructive stress. Total, unconditional acceptance of ourselves and others removes the impassable barrier to loving and being loved, and automatically enables us to enjoy truly loving relationships.

The observable reality is that practically all human relationship problems are caused by identifying people with their actions and behavior, and not acknowledging and accepting the fact that they have the innate right and freedom to say and do exactly what their unique awareness causes them to say and do. The reality is that they cannot possibly do otherwise without a different awareness, which is impossible at the instant of any decision or action. They are, however, inescapably responsible for the consequences of everything they do, refuse or neglect to do.

Value judging and resisting are irrational and totally unjustified, for the reality is that the only way we can *keep from "feeling good"* is to value judge and emotionally resist what we do not like or want!

How can we tell when we are value judging and resisting?

1. We no longer "feel good"—we experience hurting emotions and destructive stress.

2. We experience an enormous drain of our precious energy.

In order to refrain from value judging and resisting people, we must stop identifying them with their actions by realizing that they are not what they think, say or do. It is crucially important to be consciously aware that their actions are simply the means they choose to satisfy their dominant needs. This is all actions really are! Every human act is a response to our individual need to do "what we would rather do than not do"—no need, no action!

Since our fundamental human need is to "feel good," mentally, physically and emotionally, our every act is an attempt to maintain or achieve a state of "feeling good." Distorted needs breed distorted actions and behavior. Such needs stem from a distorted awareness, i.e., an awareness out of alignment with reality, with what actually IS. We can function harmoniously and effectively only to the degree that our needs are in alignment with reality, with "what actually IS," for it is impossible to deal harmoniously with unreality.

We can stop value judging and resisting ourselves and others by *realizing* that:

1. Our fundamental human need is to maintain our "feel good" and the only way we can keep from doing so is to value judge and resist people and circumstances—or to accept the value judgments of others;

2. We are not *what we do*—our actions are simply the means we choose to satisfy our dominant needs. Consequently, we aren't "bad" if we act "bad";

3. It is our unique prevailing awareness that determines "what we would rather do than not do"—we could not possibly do otherwise without a different awareness, therefore, we are invariably doing what we have to do at any given time;

4. Any fault in what we do lies not in us but in our prevailing awareness, which is not us and for which we are never to blame, in other words, there are no faulty people, only people expressing through a faulty awareness;

5. All value judgments, all "oughts," "shoulds" and "musts," are irrational for we are inevitably doing the *best* our unique awareness permits;

6. Value judging and resisting ourselves and others prevent harmonious, loving relationships, and generate hurting emotions and damaging stress;

7. Value judging is totally futile; not only does it provide no benefit, the resulting stress actually reduces our effectiveness and blocks reception of the priceless insights of our Inner Knowing;

8. Only we ourselves have the power to keep ourselves from "feeling good." No one else has that power. We do so by value judging and resisting ourselves, by accepting the value judgments of others, and by resisting unwanted circumstances.

How to accept ourselves and others "totally and unconditionally," despite unwanted characteristics, mistakes, defeats and behavior, is what the Barksdale Self-Esteem Program is all about. The basic requirement for eliminating value judging and resisting ourselves and others is to stop identifying ourselves and others with our personal characteristics, behavior, actions and awareness. False concepts of who we are and why we behave as we do, laid on us from birth by our faulty cultural conditioning, are actually the root cause of value judging and resisting one another and result in unloving relationships, hurting emotions and destructive stress.

THE SECOND STEP:
Reprogramming Your Awareness

Explanation of the Process

Everything we feel, everything we do, is a reflection of the pertinent factors of our awareness. It is impossible consciously to achieve anything we do not have an awareness of attempting. Even getting up out of a chair or moving across the room requires an awareness of accomplishing such an act—even though our intent and mental images are often on a non-conscious level.

Consequently, if we are to have more than an intellectual concept of the realities of our human behavior, we must integrate these principles and their logical implications into our awareness. Since our conditioned concepts and their *implications* are almost entirely on a non-conscious level, we must integrate these new and revised concepts into a similar level of our awareness. Only thus can we replace our faulty concepts so that we automatically act and react in alignment with "what IS."

We have found from our Foundation workshops that an effective way to do this is by verbal or mental affirmation of the new concepts and their implications while our minds are in a relaxed, quiet and receptive state. The following procedure describes how to effectively use the appropriate affirmations to achieve greater awareness and self-esteem.

The Procedure

The key word of this procedure is "*relax*," not "concentrate," for concentration induces strain. Follow the instructions and simply let yourself relax into an easy, comfortable state. For your ease and comfort, breathe normally between instructions.

Your mind is naturally in a relatively open and receptive state just before going to sleep at night and on awakening in the morning. Providing you can keep from falling asleep, you can do your affirmations while lying relaxed and comfortable in bed. This is an excellent time for most people. However, any quiet time that you can manage, even for a few minutes, can be very productive—the more often the better.

There is no need to make a "big deal" of these affirmations; the procedure is very simple. Just do them any time, and as many times during the day as you can *find* the time. Your every sincere effort will pay most welcome dividends. Naturally, the more often you do them, the sooner you will realize the results of a sound and healthy self-esteem.

Before beginning this program, it is desirable to record the following instructions and affirmations in a calm, commanding voice so that you will not be distracted by reading or trying to remember them.

Begin with the affirmations on page 45 and stay with each group until you sense they have become an integral part of your awareness, until you spontaneously act and react according to their implications.

Starting with Group 1, slowly and meaningfully repeat each affirmation three to five times at each session, depending on what you feel is best for *you*. Sense the affirmation and its implications as vividly as you can. Sense how you would feel if the statement and its implications were already fully integrated into your awareness.

Here is what to do prior to repeating the affirmations. Record these instructions too (italics are to indicate greater emphasis when speaking):

1. Take a deep breath and while inhaling stretch as hard and fully as you can possibly manage. As you begin to exhale start relaxing, and as you relax sense all your tensions, both physical and emotional, *draining away—falling away*, just as water falls off a duck.

2. Get your body into as comfortable and relaxing a position as possible. A good way is to sit erect in a straight chair with your feet flat on the floor (never cross your knees or feet), your buttocks pressed lightly against the chair back, and your head, neck and upper body in a relaxed vertical line so that you do not strain against the pull of gravity. Now take another deep breath, and while exhaling, *feel* any remaining tensions *draining away*, leaving you completely relaxed and comfortable. Imagine yourself as limp as a wet washcloth.

3. Now focus your eyes upward as far as you can without strain or discomfort, probably at about 45° or a little more. Close your eyelids lightly while maintaining your eyes in this easy upward position.

4. Now take another deep breath and while exhaling feel a deep peace flooding through your entire being. (You may like to imagine yourself in the most pleasant and relaxed situation you have ever experienced.) As you exhale, relaxing more and more all the time, imagine, deeply sense and mentally affirm, "I am *peaceful* and *relaxed.*" Repeat this exercise three times. Each time you will feel *more* peaceful and *more* relaxed, and at a *deeper* level of awareness. If you feel a still deeper level of awareness is desirable, count down slowly from ten to one. At each number, feel yourself going into a *deeper* and *deeper* level of awareness. You are now in a *completely relaxed* state, both *physically* and *mentally.*

5. Now imagine and *sense* your mind as *stilled* and *open* to new ideas. Take another deep breath and as you exhale, sense and mentally affirm, "My mind is *quiet* and *receptive.*" Do this three times. Each time your mind becomes *more quiet* and *more receptive*—even more quiet and receptive than you had thought possible. You are now so fully relaxed, physically, mentally and emotionally that your daily cares seem far away and unimportant. You are now in an exceptionally *pleasant, detached* and *receptive* state of mind.

6. Now state earnestly and confidently, "I seek greater awareness." The affirmations you will now quietly sense as you mentally repeat them (if taped, otherwise aloud) will *go deeply* into your awareness, gradually *canceling* out and *replacing* all ideas and beliefs to the contrary. You are now ready to begin your affirmations.

7. Repeat each affirmation you select from the following sets three to five times according to your personal preference.

8. After each affirmation session, count slowly from one to five to bring yourself back into your normal state of awareness. Count slowly, "One, two, three, four." Say to yourself, "At the count of five I will open my eyes and feel *relaxed* and *rested, better* than I felt before.

You will find this a very restful and energizing exercise.

Affirmations: Realities of Your Existence

Affirmations are powerful tools for programming the mind. I, myself, have achieved remarkable results and have also observed how exceptionally others have benefited from them. Some have found affirming only the "basic affirmation" to be amazingly helpful in increasing their self-esteem, especially when they identified with it and acted "as if" the affirmation were already an actuality.

Feel free to formulate your own affirmations or change these to suit your own personal needs or taste. The more comfortable you feel with an affirmation, the better it will work.

Basic Affirmation: I feel warm and loving toward myself, for I am a unique and precious being, ever doing the best my current awareness permits.

Group No. 1

1. I am solely responsible for my own life and well-being. (If I am not happy and at peace with myself, it is up to me, and me alone, to discover the causes and take appropriate action.)

2. I have the innate authority to take full charge of my own life—to think, say and do anything I choose.

3. There is a price exacted for everything I do. It is up to me to determine the price and intelligently decide whether or not I am able and willing to pay it.

4. I am inescapably responsible for everything I do, refuse or neglect to do, for I inevitably benefit or suffer according to the consequences.

5. I have the right and freedom to make mistakes, to be defeated, to fail, for I can do only as well as my prevailing awareness permits.

Group No. 2

6. My every act is a response to a personal need.

7. Both my needs and their intensity are determined by my prevailing awareness.

8. My awareness is how clearly I see, understand and evaluate, both consciously and non-consciously, *everything* that affects my life.

9. I have no cause for either pride or shame for my awareness, for it is but the automatic product of my heredity, Inner Knowing, and total life experience, none of which factors I can change on demand.

10. I can do anything I want, but what I want is determined by my awareness.

Group No. 3

11. My fundamental motivation is to "feel good," mentally, physically and emotionally—to experience a sense of inner peace and well-being.

12. My exercise of "free will" is limited by my current awareness, for I can do only what my awareness permits me to do.

13. My prevailing awareness literally dictates my every action and decision, for I can do only what my current awareness motivates me to do.

14. "Will power" is nothing more nor less than intense motivation. (I can attempt no new endeavor without sufficient motivation to give up what I am currently doing or planning to do.)

15. All "oughts," "shoulds" and "musts" are irrelevant and meaningless, for I can do only what my prevailing awareness determines I would rather do than not do.

Group No. 4

16. I am not my actions; I am the one who acts. My actions are but the means my awareness selects to fulfill my needs.

17. Since I am not my actions, I cannot possibly "prove my worth" by my actions. I am not "bad" if I act "bad."

18. I invariably do the best I can possibly do at the time.

19. There is no valid justification for condemnation. I am free of any shame, blame, guilt or remorse.

20. There is no rational justification for punishment or reward, for credit, pride or adulation. (The reward is in the "feel good" of the act, the punishment in the "feel bad.")

Group No. 5

21. Since I can do only what my awareness permits, my acts are simply "wise" or "unwise."

22. There is no "good" or "evil," only "wise" and "unwise" behavior.

23. Although I am never to blame for my actions, I am *inescapably* responsible, for I receive the consequences.

24. There is no valid basis for resistance to anything I cannot change. (Such resistance causes only turmoil and resentment.)

25. It is foolish to resent others' actions or behavior, for they can do only what their current awareness dictates.

Group No. 6

26. I can act only as harmoniously and effectively as my current awareness permits. (If I am to act "better," I must first undergo a change in my awareness.)

27. I cannot deliberately increase my awareness unless I am consciously motivated to improve it.

28. "Right" and "wrong," "fair" and "unfair" are but descriptive terms reflecting one's current awareness.

29. I have empathy and compassion for social outcasts and criminals, for everyone "has to do" what his current awareness dictates, regardless of the consequences.

30. Worry, resistance and resentment are both futile and destructive to my well-being.

Group No. 7

31. I am the center of my universe; *my* world revolves around me.

32. I am the most important, interesting and challenging person in my life.

33. The meaning and purpose of my life is the expansion of my awareness. (All my experience is but a means to this end.)

34. My fundamental responsibility in life is to increase my awareness.

35. I am a genuine "success" to the degree that I feel warm and loving toward myself.

Group No. 8

36. No one in the entire world is one iota more or less worthy than I am.

37. I have no need to "prove" myself since my very existence proves my innate worth and importance.

38. I am no less worthy or important than one with a much higher degree of awareness than I.

39. My mistakes contribute to my learning and growth. (They cannot make me feel ashamed, guilty or "less than.")

40. I can be limited only by my degree of awareness.

Group No. 9

41. No one can possibly put himself in another's place as a valid point of reference, for no one else in the entire world has the same degree of awareness.

42. Comparing myself with another's personality, conduct or accomplishments as a gauge of my worth is absolutely meaningless. (No two people have had the same heredity, Inner Knowing, and total life experience.)

43. To be motivated I must perceive desirable benefits arising from the proposed action.

44. To be wisely motivated I must determine my real need, the anticipated benefits of available alternatives, the total price demanded for each, and whether or not I am able and willing to pay it.

45. My physical well-being is of critical importance to my emotional well-being. (Otherwise I would not have the energy to support my motivation, however wise it may be.)

Group No. 10

46. I am not my awareness—I am that which is aware.

47. I am not my mind—my mind is but the human computer that receives and evaluates the data of my five senses, my instincts and intuition.

48. I am not my body—my body is but the instrument or vehicle through which I express in this material phase of my existence.

49. I am not my actions—I am that which acts. My actions are but the means I choose to fulfill my needs.

50. I am a nonphysical essence—a unique and precious being, inviolable, invincible and eternal, ever doing the best I can, ever growing in wisdom and love.

THE THIRD STEP:
Direct Action Program

Purpose

The purpose of this Direct Action Program is to:

1. Consciously generate positive feelings of self-esteem that will replace or cancel out old feelings of inferiority and inadequacy that have been accumulating at a non-conscious level since your earliest childhood;

2. Provide a new life style that generates, nourishes and maintains sound self-esteem, and that will thus make you a far happier, more effective and tranquil individual.

This action program is of vital importance. In fact, it is absolutely essential for building really sound self-esteem, for it is our self-directed constructive actions rather than our intellectual concepts, no matter how sound, that produce the positive feeling reactions required to cancel out and replace our accumulated feelings of inadequacy, inferiority and lack of worth.

In fact, if we did not have a realistic perception of how and why we behave as we do, we could still achieve a significant measure of self-esteem simply by conscientiously conforming to the following "action statements."

The most positive and direct esteem-building endeavor we can possibly undertake is to assume full responsibility for our lives, and to deliberately direct our every nonroutine thought and action, i.e., take full charge of our life and affairs, and act accordingly.

It is ironic to recognize that we actually are in charge of our own lives and affairs even now, for we cannot possibly escape the consequences of our actions. Owing, however, to our limited awareness, most of us fail by "default," by merely reacting and drifting into whatever is easiest, most attractive, readily available.

Laying out an intelligent course of action and then conscientiously following it will pay rich rewards in augmenting our self-esteem. Such self-discipline, however, can be successfully exercised only by perceiving potential benefits that will outweigh the cost involved in following such a program. We cannot actively take charge of our lives if we do not realize the benefits that would accrue from such action.

We cannot deliberately feel warm and friendly (or loving) toward ourselves like we would turn on a water faucet. We can, however, achieve this objective by not doing the things that keep us from feeling that way. Specifically, we can alert ourselves to our critical belittling and condemnatory attitudes, and conscientiously stop being so harsh and demanding with ourselves.

The following action statements are to be used in three ways:

1. First and foremost, they are to be *acted out* at every opportunity, during every day of your life. You will experience a surge of self-esteem every time you convert one from a desired action into an actuality. And, the more difficult the specific action is to accomplish, the greater your gain in self-esteem;

2. They are to be used as affirmations to reinforce and support the desired action in a manner similar to the one you used in affirming "The Realities of Your Existence";

3. They are to be used in evaluating your progress in converting a given action into a way of life. They also indicate the areas in which you need to do the most work.

Procedure

1. Choose the statement or group of statements you feel are most needed for your own growth in self-esteem. This is best done by an initial scoring of all twenty-five statements. Then, starting with the top of the list, work with each low-score statement or group of statements, as you prefer. When you can honestly score yourself a "3" or a strong "2," you are ready to proceed with the next statement or group, as the case may be.

2. Affirm your selected statement to bolster the desired action. It is usually more practical to affirm more than one statement at a time. Since they are short and direct, it is likely that you can effectively affirm five to ten statements in any one session.

   a. Before each affirmation session, earnestly and expectantly state to yourself, "I seek sound self-esteem."

   b. Vividly imagine exactly how you *would feel* if actually acting in the stated manner. Feel the victorious surge of self-esteem generated by such action. As far as possible bring all your senses into the act.

   c. Mentally rejoice in your sense of victorious accomplishment derived from taking active charge of your own life.

   d. Seize every opportunity to affirm the statement or statements on which you are currently working. Affirm any time and every time you can manage, with or without benefit of the full procedure. Every affirmation will help appreciably in accomplishing the desired action.

   e. Occasionally review all statements to fix them in your awareness better, and to ascertain where your attention and efforts are most needed.

f. Work out your own affirmation schedule, whatever is best for you personally. Actually, as you become more familiar with the program, you will be surprised at how many odd times during the day you can effectively affirm these statements. You do not need a special place or time. The main thing is to maintain your awareness of them and their importance, and to put them into *action* at every available opportunity.

Be happy and grateful for even the *slightest* evidence of improvement in your sense of self-worth. This is fully justified and of crucial importance to your success. It is progress that counts, any progress. Above all, do not be harsh and demanding with yourself.

Remember, building sound self-esteem is a three-step program, and each step is vitally important to your success. Changing your life style by making these statements the foundation of your personal and interpersonal behavior is absolutely crucial to nourishing and maintaining sound self-esteem.

CAUTION: This Direct Action Program is *not* merely an "exercise" in building esteem. It must actually become a "way of life" if you want to enjoy the rich rewards of sound self-esteem! Conformance with every statement is vital to a healthy sense of self-worth.

Action Statements

Score your compliance with these statements as follows (each score shows how true *or* the amount of time you believe that statement is true for *you*):

0 = not at all true for me
1 = somewhat true *or* true only part of the time
2 = fairly true *or* true about half the time
3 = mainly true *or* true most of the time
4 = true all of the time

Action Statements—Life Style Evaluation No. 70A

_____ 1. I accept complete responsibility for my own well-being, for everything I think, say, do and *feel.*

_____ 2. I am my own authority for everything I do, and direct my life in constructive channels.

_____ 3. I make decisions promptly and willingly accept the consequences.

_____ 4. I discipline myself through monitoring my thoughts, desires, images and expectations.

_____ 5. I think for myself and act accordingly.

_____ 6. I allow myself the freedom to make mistakes, to be "wrong," to fail, free of self-accusation, guilt or feeling "less than."

_____ 7. I take deep satisfaction in doing my work conscientiously and well.

_____ 8. I approach every problem and new endeavor with confidence.

_____ 9. I do not blame others for my problems, mistakes, defeats or handicaps.

_____ 10. I do not procrastinate or drift; I motivate myself in line with my chosen life objectives.

_____ 11. I follow all undertakings through to a logical conclusion.

_____ 12. I do not allow personal comparisons to affect my sense of worth.

_____ 13. I do not try to prove my worth by my accomplishments.

_____ 14. I defer to no one on account of wealth or status.

_____ 15. I do not blame myself for my mistakes, defeats or failures.

_____ 16. I stand up for my own values, opinions and convictions.

_____ 17. I refrain from no endeavor because of fear of failure or defeat.

_____ 18. I do not require others' confirmation or agreement and approval to do as I myself see fit.

_____ 19. I do not let others talk me into things against my better judgment.

_____ 20. I am patient, kind and gentle with myself.

_____ 21. I take the initiative in personal contacts and relationships.

_____ 22. I walk erect and face everyone with a friendly countenance.

_____ 23. I do not deny my needs, feelings or opinions to please others.

_____ 24. I am frank and open with everyone, free of all masks and pretensions.

_____ 25. I do not try to impress others with my worth or importance.

_____ **YOUR LIFE STYLE INDEX or LSI (sum of scores for all statements)**

The possible range of Life Style Indexes is from 0 to 100. The higher your score, the more your life style is in accord with the realities of human behavior.

Further Thoughts on Self-Esteem

Our Natural State of Being

Our natural state of being is inner peace and joy for our many blessings, for the beauty and wonder all about us. But when we are absorbed in our own problems, in our feelings of inadequacy, inferiority and lack of worth, we are too involved and tense to perceive the "goodness" of life. The utter simplicity of life is itself our greatest block to appreciation and understanding, for due to our lack of a sense of importance and "realness," we have a need for complexity and turmoil to assure us that we really are alive, i.e., "I 'hurt,' therefore I am."

Good and Evil

There is nothing inherently evil or malevolent in life. There are only the consequences of our wise or unwise acts, be they "good" or "bad," harmonious or inharmonious. The law of cause and effect is immutable; "as ye sow so shall ye reap." "Sin" is no more than a synonym for a mistake, and "evil" no more than its inharmonious consequence. Our only basic problem in life is our *lack of awareness!*

Human Nature vs. Human Conditioning

One of our greatest challenges in self-exploration is to determine how much of our behavior is due to "human conditioning." We can change our conditioning through the motivation induced by clear understanding, but human nature is not so easily changed. Fortunately, when we really look we will find that adverse behavior is almost entirely due to faulty conditioning. The better aspects of behavior, such as our deep need to love and be loved, to be "good," to commune with our creator, are part of our "human nature." Greed, hate, compulsive competition, arrogance and aggression are typical products of our human conditioning.

Responsibility

No matter our misfortunes, handicaps or how much we have been kicked around, we are still responsible for our individual lives and well-being. It is up to us; the choice is ours, and despite wishful thinking, we can only start from *where we are*. It is not what has happened to us that is of paramount importance. It is what we do about what happens to us that determines our degree of well-being.

One's limited and distorted awareness does not constitute "permission" or a license to commit immoral, antisocial or destructive acts—it merely *explains* the nature and origin of these acts. Understanding the basic cause of such acts permits us to focus our awareness on the crux of the problem, and thus better equips us to deal effectively with the particular situation.

Character

A person's character is but an outward manifestation of his state of awareness. Thus, a "strong character" merely means that one's awareness is such that the motivations generated by it are harmonious, constructive, and highly acceptable to society. On the other hand, the motivations stemming from the limited and distorted awareness of a "weak character" tend to be inharmonious, ineffective, destructive, and unacceptable by society's arbitrary and often unrealistic standards.

Self-discipline

Self-discipline is a matter of motivating oneself to do what seems to be desirable according to one's values. If weighing the pros and cons of a desirable action does not motivate a person, it is better to deliberately decide to forego the particular action and pay whatever price is demanded by refusal. Otherwise, effectiveness and self-esteem are handicapped by indecision, conflict and self-recrimination.

The "Easy Way"

Although self-rejection can generate an intense, driving motivation to achieve surpassing wealth, power and prestige, due to a compulsive need to prove oneself "better than," there is an "easy way" to material success, a way that is more rewarding and less damaging to the individual and society, but equally effective. Everyone has deep, innate urges to express, to fulfill potential talents and capabilities. These urges can be satisfied harmoniously and effectively when one is free of the crippling emotional tensions and blind spots that stem from self-hate and rejection. One *can* achieve prosperity and respect without the fierce, aggressive competition that breeds high blood pressure, ulcers and migraine headaches, without neglecting inner needs, without alienation from others—by achieving a greater awareness and a healthy self-esteem.

Identification with Our Actions

We are free to make mistakes without self-recrimination, without feeling "less than," only when we stop identifying with our actions, when we realize that our actions are simply the means our limited awareness chooses for fulfilling our needs and objectives. When we fully accept the fact that we are *not* our actions, we realize that no personal achievement can make us "better than" others and no defeat or failure can make us "less than" others.

Inner Freedom

The most precious "freedom" is *inner* freedom, which arises from realizing who we are, how and why we function as we do, and what is actually of ultimate significance in our lives.

Humility

Humility is the ability to accomplish things without taking credit for them. It stems from realizing that we can do only what our prevailing awareness enables and motivates us to do, and that our awareness is

59

but the automatic product of our individual heredity, Inner Knowing, and total life experience. A truly humble person has no need to say, or even think, "I am humble."

Reward

The reward is in the act. If the self-satisfaction and gratification, the "feel good" derived from a given action, are insufficient reward, a person will feel disappointed, even cheated, if not repaid in kind. However, if one wants to be a free and independent individual, it behooves him to find reward in the action itself or refrain from such action. Otherwise, the "giver" is no freer than a "receiver" who has a compulsive need to return the favor.

Importance of Physical Health

We often overlook the vital importance of health and physical fitness to our overall well-being. The fact is that a high degree of energy is essential, both for optimum decision making and for implementing our constructive motivations. No matter how exemplary one's desires may be, they count for little if the individual does not have the energy and stamina to carry them out. Moreover, emotional depression can result from simply becoming overly fatigued.

Value Judging

The greatest handicap to harmonious human relationships, marital or otherwise, is our tendency to impose our values on others, and then to become resentful or angry because they, due to their different awareness, are unable to comply. Nothing precludes open communication or destroys potentially meaningful relationships like value judgments.

Resistance and Resentment

Resistance and resentment result from the inability to recognize and accept the reality of the moment, and like worry and fear, they are both futile and destructive. Would you resist the rising of the sun and resent that it will not stop in its appointed course?

Letting Go

When we can let go and "let it happen," it not only takes the sting out of grief and other unwanted experiences, it also releases the tensions that prevent us from "tuning in" to the inner wisdom ever waiting on the threshold of our consciousness.

We Describe Ourselves

We unconsciously describe our own negative characteristics when we are critical of others, for we see in them those qualities we most dislike in ourselves. This principle operates in our puritannical moralizing. When we point the finger at another, three of our fingers point back to ourselves.

Self-acceptance

We cannot be genuinely kind and loving to others when we are harsh and demanding of ourselves. How can we accept others when we cannot approve of and accept ourselves? Without self-acceptance we can only express our inner turmoil and pain. How can we have a peaceful society when we are at war within ourselves? Does not one's countenance often resemble a battlefield?

Parenting

"Reward and punishment" are extremely simple and easy ways to raise children. However, our children pay a price they can ill afford for such raising. Since reward and punishment literally force us to identify with our actions, we cannot help but feel inferior and unworthy whenever we make a mistake. Taking the time and effort to advise our offspring of the costs and benefits of the alternatives available for meeting their specific needs or objectives, then allowing them to make their own decisions (within their current capabilities), and finally allowing them to accept the consequences of their decisions, involves some risk and *is* considerably more difficult and time-consuming. This method, however, pays rich dividends, for it builds self-reliance and self-esteem. Sound self-esteem is the most precious gift parents can give their children.

Self-sufficiency

Every time we do something for others that they are capable of doing for themselves, we literally *steal* from their self-esteem. The more we love a person, the more it behooves us to see that we do not cheat him of any opportunity to benefit from *thinking* and *doing* for himself, even though he may suffer defeat and physical and/or emotional pain in the process.

Emotional Dependency

We cannot live another's life or bear another's burdens, no matter how great our love and care. The best thing parents can do for their children is to release them emotionally, allow them to become whole, self-reliant people, free of binding emotional dependency. The basic responsibility of parents is to assist their children in making a smooth transition from being utterly dependent as infants to being strong, self-reliant individuals when they leave the nest.

Moral Admonitions

Moral values can be used as guides for the less aware, but when we beat ourselves and others "over the head" with them, we cause only destructive guilt, self-rejection and rebellion. Rather than indulging in moral admonitions, it is much more constructive simply to explain to the individual the advantages of acting in the desired "moral" manner, and then allow him the freedom to act as he himself sees fit. He will then benefit from the consequences, even if they are "bad," for instead of inducing guilt in a person who is not motivated to comply with a particular moral admonition, this procedure will actually enhance his self-esteem. In this way we can encourage "moral" action without damaging the individual's self-esteem. The most effective teacher is one who teaches by setting an example rather than by words.

Self-realization

When we stop identifying with our actions, we realize that our very existence proves our worth and importance in the scheme of things. We realize that we cannot be one *iota* more or less worthy, more or less important, than anyone else. Is not the "dignity of humanity" rooted in this realization?

Our Learning and Growth

Our every experience contributes to our learning and growth. When we are hurting the most we are growing the most because we are motivated to seek new solutions in order to avoid our discomfort. Sometimes our growth is on an "incubating" level rather than a conscious level.

Releasing Emotional Turmoil

If, when we are anxious, frustrated, discouraged or defeated, we can pause to contemplate what is of ultimate importance in our lives, all our problems will fall into place, and our fears and worries will shrink to their true size and relative importance.

"Me and Mine"

When we recognize that we are nonphysical essences, we realize that the word "mine" can only denote "stewardship." Otherwise we would take "it" with us when we die. What *can* we take with us other than an expanded awareness?

Arguments

An "argument" is a demand for confirmation and agreement, whereas a "discussion" is the sharing of information and opinions.

Loneliness

Loneliness is primarily an effect of low self-esteem, of trying to avoid or escape from facing and communicating with a self we dislike and reject. When we feel truly warm and friendly toward ourselves, when we genuinely appreciate our innate worth and uniqueness, we enjoy being with ourselves, even for protracted periods. Then, instead of berating ourselves for our lack of worth and importance, our mistakes, defeats and shortcomings, we communicate with our inner self as an old and valued friend.

An Ordered Universe

When we look up at the sky on a clear night we see perfect order as the heavenly bodies proceed on their appointed courses. Astronomers can predict the exact movement of the planets for hundreds of years. If there is chaos and happenstance here on earth, exactly at what level or altitude does the transition to harmony take place? Can we have perfect order in the heavens and chaos on earth—must it not be all one or the other? Is it not our mistakes and lack of awareness manifesting through the immutable law of cause and effect that generate our seeming happenstance and chaos? And, if there is order, must there not *also* be purpose?

What Happened in the Interim?

Did you ever stop to think, when viewing a mean and embittered countenance, what has transpired in that person's life to effect such a change from an originally sweet and lovable infant? Has it not been largely the effect of faulty conditioning and the resulting destruction of natural self-esteem?

Periodic Evaluation of Your Progress

To determine your "current" degree of self-esteem, check your progress by scoring yourself approximately every week on the Self-Esteem Evaluation. If you are conscientious and diligent in your efforts on all three steps, you will be pleasantly surprised at your progress.

A periodic check of your progress in building self-esteem will prove to be a distinct help. Any evidence of progress will motivate you to keep working, learning and growing.

This program, if followed in its entirety, will create a life style that generates, nourishes and maintains sound self-esteem, thus ensuring a harmonious, productive and happy life for you.

Conclusion

We are responsible for our individual lives. We have been imbued with a deep urge to express goodness and love, and have been granted "free will" and the immutable law of cause and effect to lead us into ever greater awareness—so that we can free ourselves of ignorance and self-imposed bondage—so that we can each become a whole person, a serene, self-loving individual who truly "loves his neighbor as *himself*."

What we do with our lives is up to each of us, whether we live in "fear and trembling," in self-loathing and misery, or whether we embark on an ever more exciting and rewarding adventure, free of false and distorted concepts, conflict, futility and frustration, of the inhibiting and debilitating emotional turmoil of a crippling self-esteem.

In sum, we will achieve sound self-esteem to the degree that we realize the following: that we each have the sole responsibility, the authority, freedom and ability to direct our own lives and affairs as we see fit; that people are innately "good," worthy and important, nonphysical essences, unique and precious beings; and that at our divine center each of us is inviolable, invincible and eternal; that no matter how badly we may err, how much we may stumble or slip backward in our tortuous upward climb, we are each an inseparable part of a Common Source, varying only in our awareness; that regardless how slow and uneven the rate, we are each ever growing in wisdom and love; and that we have all the time there is for our unfoldment—and that all our experience is but a means to this end.

The acid test for truly high self-esteem is this: Do you, when you occasionally happen to focus your awareness on yourself, spontaneously experience a subtle surge of warmth and love, as you do perhaps when you pause to think lovingly of your sweetheart, spouse or child? If you do, however fleeting this sense of warmth and love toward *yourself* may be, you are one of those rare individuals who has a genuine appreciation and regard for your own intrinsic worth.

APPENDIX

Also Available in Spanish

This book and the self-esteem evaluation in it are also available in Spanish, as is *Taking Charge of My Life: Choices, Changes and Me*, a book for teens and preteens. They may be obtained from The Barksdale Foundation. You will find the Foundation's address and phone number at the end of this section.

Study Groups

If you are unable to attend a Self-Esteem Workshop, or wish to supplement your workshop training, if you have enjoyed reading this book and want to share its content with others, consider starting a Study Group for Building Self-Esteem.

A special packet is available for self-led study groups. This packet contains *Building Self-Esteem* as the basic text, with a *Study Guide for Building Self-Esteem* that covers the material in thirteen 2-hour sessions. Also included is an affirmation tape, a Pocket Companion of daily lessons and affirmations to carry with you, Self-Esteem and Life Style Evaluations, and Progress Charts. Each person in the group will need one of these packets.

To lead or join a group, you don't have to know a lot about self-esteem, for you will all learn together. The leader simply follows the detailed directions for organizing the group and for conducting the sessions as outlined in the *Study Guide*.

Participation in a study group can be stimulating and enjoyable—a most rewarding experience for those who will take the initiative to organize the group, as well as for those who join it. These study sessions can actually change your life and the lives of those around you by making you a happier, more integrated and effective human being!

This group work, of course, is not intended to replace the conventional techniques of psychotherapy and other forms of professional counseling. People with serious emotional problems are advised to consult a competent professional.

Additional Self-Esteem and Stress Control Materials Available

If you would like to know more about The Barksdale Foundation and its Self-Esteem and Stress Control materials, call or write for a catalog of visual and audio products for adults, teens and preteens.

The Barksdale Foundation
P.O. Box 187
Idyllwild, CA 92549
Tel: (909) 659-4676

Thought Provoking Books
for Expanding Your Awareness

Title   **Author**

The Prophet .... Kahlil Gibran

All That You Are .... Mary

Jonathan Livingston Seagull .... Richard Bach

A Search for Truth .... Ruth Montgomery

Breakthrough to Creativity .... Shafica Karagulla

I Say Sunrise .... Talbot Mundy

*Psychic Discoveries behind
the Iron Curtain* .... Ostrander & Schroeder

Handbook to Higher Consciousness .... Ken Keyes, Jr.

The Book .... Alan Watts

The Unobstructed Universe .... Stewart Edward White

Many Wonderful Things ..... Robert H. Huffman & Irene Specht

Divine Healing of Mind and Body .... Murdo MacDonald-Bayne

Love Letters from Spirit to You .... Jacob Beilhart

Spirit Fruit and Voice .... Jacob Beilhart

There Is a River .... Thomas Sugrue

Many Lifetimes .... Denys Kelsey & Joan Grant

Illusions .... Richard Bach

The Art of Selfishness .... David Seabury